be honored than those who produce them; for art of living well.” – Aristotle

Library of Congress Control Number
ISBN: 9798986841342
LCCN: 2023945558
Printed in China
Designed by Mehrab Meraj
First Artvoices Books Publishing edition 2024
Artvoices Books Publishing
www.artvoicesbooks.com

Special **Thank You** to Yee Wong

Notes To My Daughter

Affirmations, Empowerment, & Hope

TERRY SMITH

Dedicated to My Daughter Maya

Notes To My Daughter is especially for young brown girls. To achieve anything of real value in this life, you must believe you are deserving and worth it. If you can see yourself living the dream, then you can manifest destiny, but first you must believe in yourself.

This book comes from the unconditional love a father has for his daughter. My highest expectations for her living her best life. A written guide for girls that will empower, transform and transition them into womanhood knowing they are powerful, intelligent, and enough.

Notes To My Daughter encourages girl power and women's empowerment. This book features profiles of influential and groundbreaking Black and Latin women who have set the precedent and are proof that anything is possible.

Notes To My Daughter is an insightful, and powerful book that will instill in your little girl that she is the masterpiece of her life and nothing is beyond her reach. We co-exist in a society that's male dominated, openly racist, sexist, and misogynistic toward women, especially of color and this book is much needed tool to assist girls in maintaining self-respect and high self-esteem.

Women in the 21st century continue to fight and advocate for their basic rights as a woman and this book will ensure the next generation is cut from the same fabric. Our daughters need positive reinforcement and support more now than ever. This book is a testament to that narrative.

This book will create an unbreakable bond between minority parents and their daughters who are mostly from lower income households and marginalized communities.

Parents absence because of work or school throughout their child's informative years will negatively affect them emotionally, physically, and mentally. This is the primary reason for the lack of success in the child's life. **Notes To My Daughter** will be a positive reinforcement to establish a foundation of positivity and self-worth.

Social media and Hollywood are co-parenting our children without their best intentions. This book will give parents and daughters a failsafe plan. **Notes To My Daughter** offer parents a tool to offset the negative and influential effects of societal norms and social media with positive affirmations and role models of the girl's ethnic background. **Notes To My Daughter** reinforces positive messaging that we want our daughters to embrace.

Notes To My Daughter is essential for parents and their daughters to affirm who they are, who they can be, and encourage them to believe in themselves.

Affirmations from **Notes To My Daughter** are spoken aloud between the parent and the child on a daily basis. In turn the *affirmations* in **Notes To My Daughter** become embedded in the subconscious realms and overtime replace the negative beliefs with positive thoughts and or actions instilling confidence, positivity and ambition.

–Terry Smith

Notes To My Daughter

Affirmations, Empowerment, & Hope

TERRY SMITH

"Never dwell on the past because each day
possibilities."

will bring a new set of opportunities and
– Terry Smith

BEYONCE

"I can never be safe;
I always try and go
against the grain. As soon
as I accomplish one thing,
I just set a higher goal.
That's how I've gotten to
where I am."

I AM AN SINGER, I AM A WOMAN

SHAKIRA

"I feel like there is a part of me that represents a minority in the U.S., a minority around the world. People who struggle, people who want to succeed with drive and ambition."

I AM AN SINGER, I AM A WOMAN

Always remember you are the sum of your thoughts.

If you think or believe you won’t win, you will lose.

If you believe you’re not good enough, you’ve convinced yourself you’re not.

A quitter will never succeed.

Never give in to doubt, fear or weakness.

To achieve your goals, you must have a plan and then execute.

VIOLA DAVIS

"I tell my daughter every morning, 'Now, what are the two most important parts of you?' And she says, 'My head and my heart.' Because that's what I've learned in the foxhole: What gets you through life is strength of character and strength of spirit and love."

I AM AN ACTRESS, I AM A WOMAN

SALMA HAYEK

"I have never denied my background or my culture. I have taught my child to embrace her Mexican heritage, to love my first language, Spanish, to learn about Mexican history, music, folk art, food, and even the Mexican candy I grew up with."

I AM AN ACTRESS, I AM A WOMAN

In life you will encounter obstacles that require navigation through the power of thought process.

Life is a steady stream of interactions between the conscious and the unconscious.

Not every problem has a logical answer.

You can do it only if you put in the work.

Never be too concerned with the thoughts, opinions, and actions of others.

You can't control anyone but your own behavior, thoughts, and words.

DR. REBECCA LEE CRUMPLER

"I early conceived a liking for and sought every opportunity to relieve the sufferings of others."

I AM A DOCTOR, I AM A WOMAN

DR. HELEN RODRIGUEZ TRIAS

"We need health, but above all we need to create a grounding for healthy public policy that redresses and salvages the growing inequities. We cannot achieve a healthier us without achieving a healthier, more equitable health care system, and ultimately, a more equitable society."

I AM A DOCTOR, I AM A WOMAN

You must hold yourself to the highest standards.

Every human being is born with a purpose. If they accomplish their mission in this life is entirely up to them.

Always focus on yourself and block out all fear, doubt, and negativity.

Distractions are counterproductive and keep you from achieving a higher level of enlightenment.

Life is to be taken seriously. It's not a joke, and it's not easy. It's simple and completely complicated and if you're not careful everyday will be a constant struggle, unrelenting and unforgivable.

In life, you will need a strategy to be victorious.

KARA WALKER

"I guess there was a little bit of a slight rebellion, maybe a little bit of a renegade desire that made me realize at some point in my adolescence that I really liked pictures that told stories of things - genre paintings, historical paintings - the sort of derivatives we get in contemporary society."

I AM AN ARTIST, I AM A WOMAN

FRIDA KAHLO

"Since my subjects have always been my sensations, my states of mind and the profound reactions that life has been producing in me, I have frequently objectified all this in figures of myself, which were the most sincere and real thing that I could do in order to express what I felt inside and outside of myself."

You must always keep your eye on the prize.

You will achieve all you want in this life if you make the right decisions and learn from your mistakes.

You must be prepared for life's obstacles, the seen and unseen.

If you work hard, with a little luck your dreams will become reality.

You must listen in between the lines that are not spoken.

You will not be perfect and fail some test but always revisit what you answered incorrectly so you don't repeat the mistakes.

OPRAH WINFREY

"Think like a queen. A queen is not afraid to fail. Failure is another steppingstone to greatness."

I AM AN ENTREPRENEUR, I AM A WOMAN

MARÍA ASUNCIÓN ARAMBURUZABALA

"I am convinced that the women's sector has capabilities, but it is also required to break with many taboos and myths from within the family."

Always strive to overachieve in your studies for this work ethic is fundamental to forecast your future success.

Close your eyes and imagine yourself living the life you want. If you can see it, you can be it.

A test reveals what we have learned and where we need to refocus.

Never be scared to be tested. The only person who fears a test is the one who is not prepared.

Life is a process, essential for you to sustain.

The World is equal parts ugly and beautiful.

CONSTANCE BAKER MOTLEY

"I rejected the notion that my race or sex would bar my success in life."

I AM A LAWYER, I AM A WOMAN

CARMEN ORTIZ

"..don't let other people or obstacles limit your growth; be determined to defy the odds. Don't limit yourself by what other people may perceive you as; they don't know you. Don't be afraid to show and demonstrate who you are."

I AM A LAWYER, I AM A WOMAN

In life there is a constant struggle regarding good versus evil.

Weak people will attempt to convince you they are stronger than you. It's strategic not to respond with ego but with tact.

Pretending to be weak when you're strong and strong when you're weak will always give you the advantage over your opponent. It will lure them into a false sense of security which is a façade.

Overconfidence could be detrimental to your downfall.

Feel compassion for hateful people because they have been conditioned and brainwashed to hate.

Work smarter, not harder, and everything in life is attainable.

SONYA SOTOMAYOR

"So many people grew up with challenges, as I did. There weren't always happy things happening to me or around me. But when you look at the core of goodness within yourself - at the optimism and hope - you realize it comes from the environment you grew up in."

I AM A JUDGE, I AM A WOMAN

KETANJI BROWN JACKSON

"It has taken 232 years and 115 prior appointments for a Black woman to be selected to serve on the Supreme Court of the United States, but we've made it! We've made it — all of us."

I AM A JUDGE, I AM A WOMAN

Always expect the unexpected.

Never talk about who you are, let your actions show the World who you are.

I'm so fortunate and blessed to have you as my daughter.

You give my life purpose and meaning.

Never forget to be thankful for what you have, not what you don't have.

Fill your life with an abundance of laughter, kindness, and generosity.

ANGELA DAVIS

"I think the importance of doing activist work is precisely because it allows you to give back and to consider yourself not as a single individual who may have achieved whatever but to be a part of an ongoing historical movement."

I AM AN ACTIVIST, I AM A WOMAN

DOLORES HUERTA

"We do need women in civic life. We do need women to run for office, to be in political office. We need a feminist to be at the table when decisions are being made so that the right decisions will be made."

I AM AN ACTIVIST, I AM A WOMAN

You are my love, my life, my daughter.

You are a strong, beautiful, smart, loving, generous, kind, and honest.

I see your true and vast potential.

People are like plants, and flowers, how you care for them matters. Your words and actions will either give them life or cause their demise.

Be careful who you offend and who attempts to offend you.

Never be defined by what others think of you.

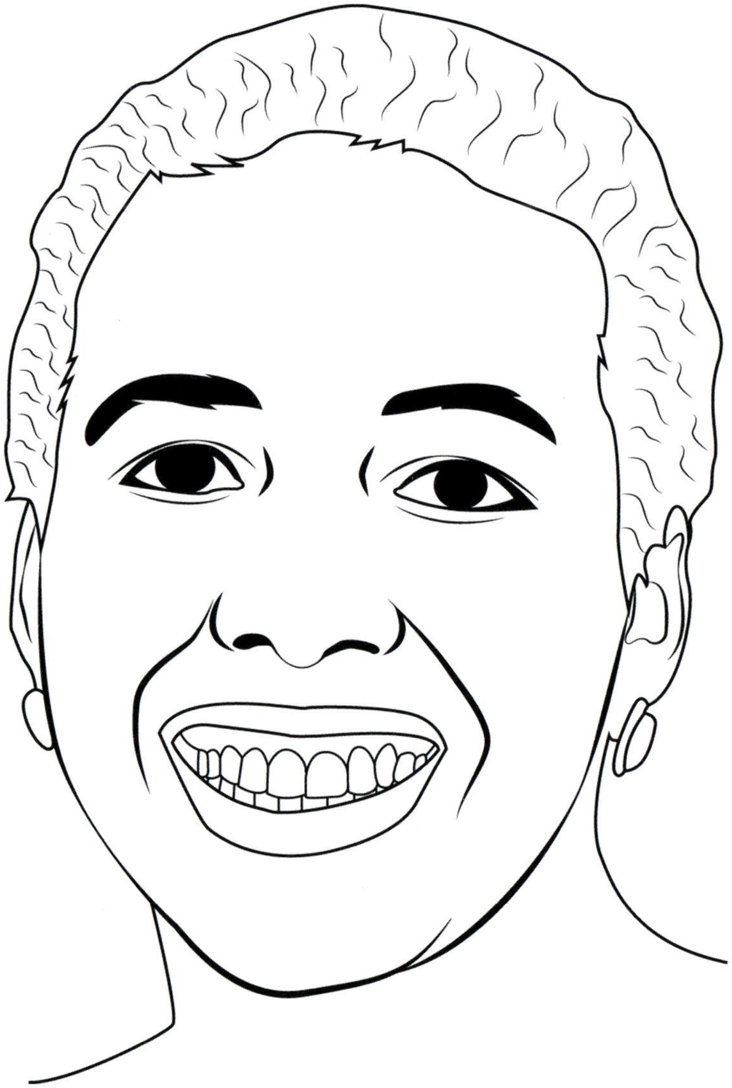

DR. BEVERLY DANIEL TATUM

"To work effectively as an agent of change in a pluralistic society, it is necessary to be able to connect with people different from oneself."

I AM A PSYCOLOGIST, I AM A WOMAN

MARTHA E. BERNAL, PH.D

"Throughout my life, however critical I might be of this country, I have felt grateful for the opportunities of which I availed myself. They would most likely not have existed had I lived in Mexico."

I AM A PSYCOLOGIST, I AM A WOMAN

Hurt people, will always hurt people because it’s their defense mechanism.

I believe without any question of doubt, you will change the World for the better.

You are an old soul and knowledgeable beyond your years.

I'm so happy you picked me to be your father.

You are the best of me, and you are loved.

Never put off for tomorrow what can be accomplished today.

ALEXANDRIA OCASIO-CORTEZ

"Mentors of mine were under a big pressure to minimize their femininity to make it. I'm not going to do that. That takes away my power. I'm not going to compromise who I am."

I AM A POLITICIAN, I AM A WOMAN

KAMALA HARRIS

"Here's the thing: every office I've run for I was the first to win. First person of color. First woman. First woman of color. Every time."

I AM A POLITICIAN, I AM A WOMAN

You are the pride of our ancestors and their dreams manifested.

Always stay true to you and who you are and how you want to be perceived in the World.

Loving you, and being loved by you, unconditionally, is the greatest gift I have ever given and received.

To be a great leader, you first must be a great listener.

Take your time and never rush to judgment.

Respect elders who are wise, experienced, and can teach you valuable lessons in life.

MARIA ELENA SALINAS

"A misinformed or under-informed society is very vulnerable to the abuse of those in power. So let's remember we are the only filter between those in power and those they are trying to reach or those they are trying to control, so we can't let anybody intimidate us."

I AM A JOURNALIST, I AM A WOMAN

JOY REID

"I always want to be doing something - going somewhere, doing a project, teaching a class, writing an article. I try to use up my day. You have a limited time on this planet - try to use as much of it as you can for productive purposes."

I AM A JOURNALIST, I AM A WOMAN

You are the only person you can trust 100%. Always listen to your inner voice and your gut. Never go against your intuitive, and instinctual voice.

Communication is the key to an amicable result.

Make decisions based on rationality and logic, never emotions.

Never diagnose someone by their symptoms alone. Examine the root of the problem as the cause of the symptoms and dispense prescription accordingly.

Life is a marathon, not a race.

Every moment, decision, defines your life.

ANN LOWE

"All the pleasure I have had, I owe to sewing."

I AM A FASHION DESIGNER, I AM A WOMAN

CAROLINA HERRERA

"Fashion is a dream. It's difficult, and there are many aspects of fashion that are very difficult, but if you love it like I do, because I really have a passion, now, for fashion, it's not easy, but nothing is easy in life."

I AM A FASHION DESIGNER, I AM A WOMAN

Look deep inside your soul for the answers to the tough questions. Never allow yourself to be manipulated and or coerced into believing what is irrational and analogical.

Care for the health and well-being of others, especially those you love.

Never assume you know everything.

Take your time, access the problem, set the equation, and apply the solution.

I'm your Dad, I will teach you essential life lessons allowing you a chance to live your best life.

It’s OK not to know everything but it’s not OK not to try.

ELLEN OCHOA

“I think of it as a good opportunity to let in particular, school kids, know that this job and other interesting jobs in science and engineering are open to anyone who works hard in school and gets a good education and studies math and science. And that it’s not just for a select group of people.”

I AM AN ASTRONAUT, I AM A WOMAN

MAE CAROL JEMISON

"Never be limited by other people's limited imaginations...If you adopt their attitudes, then the possibility won't exist because you'll have already shut it out...You can hear other people's wisdom, but you've got to re-evaluate the world for yourself."

I AM AN ASTRONAUT, I AM A WOMAN

You are born alone, and you will die, alone.

The in-between time you spend in search for your true self will define you.

You are the best version of me.

Anything and everything in moderation.

Love your life, live to love and love to live.

Life is filled with uncertainty, but you must trust your instincts.

MISTY COPELAND

"I think most people think of ballerinas as kind of either as a fairytale, far-away thing that's really not attainable, something they can't grasp, or they think of them as European or Russian and kind of their nose up in the air. So, it's cool for me to, like, sit with them and for them to really see themselves as me."

I AM A BALLERINA, I AM A WOMAN

EVELYN CISNEROS-LEGATE

"My grandparents all emigrated here from Mexico. We were always told and expected to act as role models for the country of Mexico. I think it served us so well, I was always so sensitive, especially to the little ones who were brown like me."

I AM A BALLERINA, I AM A WOMAN

Take one step at a time and never lose sight of what's in front of you.

Take your time in hopes of doing it correctly the first time.

It’s important to know your past but don’t live in the past, live for today and dream about tomorrow.

You must forgive all those who hurt you and meant you harm. Do not harbor anger or resentment and wish them ill will because we're all connected.

Communication, passion, vision, preparation, courage, perseverance integrity and organization are the keys to success.

Stay focused and stay in your lane.

SERENA WILLIAMS

"Luck has nothing to do with it, because I have spent many, many hours, countless hours, on the court working for my one moment in time, not knowing when it would come."

I AM AN ATHLETE, I AM A WOMAN

NANCY LOPEZ

"A competitor will find a way to win. Competitors take bad breaks and use them to drive themselves just that much harder. Quitters take bad breaks and use them as reasons to give up. It's all a matter of pride."

People change. Their change doesn't mean they're not who they were. It only means they have changed. We can still love them for the moments we shared and the memories, but we must move on before the language becomes disdainful, hurtful, and disrespectful.

Be proud of your imperfections.

We are on this Earth to experience. Each person has a unique dynamic. In the end you will not be judged.

No fear of the unknown.

You are my heart. Everything I do is for you. No one means more to me than you.

Power of thought and mind over matter are essential to physical, emotional, and mental well-being.

KATHERINE JOHNSON

"Girls are capable of doing everything men are capable of doing. Sometimes they have more imagination than men."

I AM A SCIENTIST, I AM A WOMAN

SABRINA GONZALEZ PASTERSKI

"When I want to motivate myself to do more, like, if there's a particular task that I want to do but haven't been able to do it, and I see that someone else has done it, I think 'If they can do it, I can do it."

You must know when to embrace change.

Listen to your inner voice.

Your laughter is glorious, harmonious, and infectious. It's a constant reminder how happiness, love, and care lives inside of you.

The World is your playground but if you're not careful it could turn into your prison.

Don't be concerned with the words, thoughts, and actions of others unless it directly and or indirectly affects you.

Stay the course and the universe will guide you to your destination.

FRIDA ESCOBEDO

"…I would like to be a congruous person, a person that is aware of the time and place she lives in. I try to remember that not only as an architect but also as an individual. The tiny, everyday actions are the ones I feel can have more impact."

I AM AN ARCHITECT, I AM A WOMAN

NORMA MERRICK SKLAREK

"Architecture should be working on improving the environment of people in their homes, in their places of work, and their places of recreation. It should be functional and pleasant, not just in the image of the architect's ego."

Girls are as strong or stronger than boys. Never believe you are the weaker sex.

You and I have known each other since the beginning of time. When this life comes to an end we will find each other again, and again in perpetuity.

For those who do not attempt to better themselves and strive for a better quality of life will be haunted and plagued by the thought of what if.

Always be a person of your word because your reputation is paramount.

Never lie or be dishonest unless it's a matter of living a better quality of life or death.

Your word is your currency.

THELMA GOLDEN

“The privilege I’ve had as a curator is not just the discovery of new works... but what I’ve discovered about myself and what I can offer in the space of an exhibition - to talk about beauty, to talk about power, to talk about ourselves, and to talk and speak to each other.”

I AM A CURATOR, I AM A WOMAN

MARCELA GUERRERO

"You have to do a lot of work to repair years of (Latino art) being forgotten, and it's a little overwhelming."

I AM A CURATOR, I AM A WOMAN

Be a person that can be trusted, respectful and has significant value.

Always see the beauty in everything and everyone.

Never judge people by their education, or appearance.

Judge people by their character, actions, and words.

Your health is more important than anything in your life.

Without health, you have nothing.

GEISHA WILLIAMS

"I'd like to see a world where there are so many Latina women leaders - and women of all different backgrounds - in the top jobs around the country. When that happens, we've succeeded."

I AM A CEO, I AM A WOMAN

ROSALIND BREWER

"I want young girls to realize that the possibilities are big. They can be race car drivers. They can be astronauts. They can be CEOs."

I AM A CEO, I AM A WOMAN

Always remember to take very good care of yourself.

Your future is in full view for all to see.

Never settle for less, and always strive for excellence.

You get out what you put in. Always 110%.

Always dream, but no dream is possible without hard work, belief, passion, and commitment.

You are young, gifted, and talented.

KEECHANT SEWELL

"When you are no pushover, you will be called difficult. When you do things your own way – 'You don't listen, you are paranoid.' Your very existence is a problem for many."

I AM A POLICE COMMISIONER, I AM A WOMAN

MAGDA FERNANDEZ

"There were a lot of challenges being female but also being a Hispanic female….I know times have changed, but you had to work harder, you had to prove yourself more."

I AM A POLICE COMMISIONER, I AM A WOMAN

There are no third chances for anyone that has lied or deceived you.

Your friendship should be earned and rewarded.

Always tell the truth no matter the consequences.

Never want to be anyone but you.

You are on this planet for a purpose.

Believe you can, and you will. See yourself where you want to be, and you will be.

MARÍA TERAS ARNAL

"When as a professional you learn to know yourself and understand what you are good at, you can find your magical place."

I AM AN ENGINEER, I AM A WOMAN

MARY JACKSON

"Every time we get to the finish line, they move it. Every time."

I AM AN ENGINEER, I AM A WOMAN

Never let anyone have power over you.

Stand with the power of truth and you will never be defeated.

This World is not fair.

There are people who can only communicate in conflict, and they should be avoided at all costs.

You are a champion.

You are defined by your decisions.

BELL HOOKS

"Once you do away with the idea of people as fixed, static entities, then you see that people can change, and there is hope. Any society based on domination supports and condones violence. I will not have my life narrowed down. I will not bow down to somebody else's whim or to someone else's ignorance."

I AM A PHILOSOPHER, I AM A WOMAN

GLORIA ANZALDÚA

"A woman who writes has power, and a woman with power is feared. I change myself; I change the world. By writing I put order in the world, give it a handle so I can grasp it."

I AM A PHILOSOPHER, I AM A WOMAN

You are the definition of humanity.

Never be afraid of the unknown.

We must overcome our fears and embrace our phobias.

Your health is paramount; your body is a temple.

This is the start of a new week, to work on who you are destined to be.

Push yourself, know no limits.

RITA PIERSON

“Every child deserves a champion—an adult who will never give up on them, who understands the power of connection, and insists that they become the best that they can possibly be. I gave [my students] a saying to say: ‘I am somebody. I was somebody when I came. I’ll be a better somebody when I leave.”

I AM AN EDUCATOR, I AM A WOMAN

ELSA SALAZAR CADE

"I greatly appreciate that I was able to get to where I am now because of public schools, and my teachers."

I AM AN EDUCATOR / I AM A WOMAN

One day you will reap the fruit of your commitment, dedication, and hard work.

You inspire me to be a better man, human and father.

We all start at the beginning and strive to finish hard.

For some, there is only one chance, one choice.

You are the prettier, smarter, younger, stronger version of me.

Never pick anyone over your studies, or family.

MAYA ANGELOU

"I have great respect for the past. If you don't know where you've come from, you don't know where you're going. I have respect for the past, but I'm a person of the moment. I'm here, and I do my best to be completely centered at the place I'm at, then I go forward to the next place."

I AM A POET, I AM A WOMAN

ADA LIMON

"There are so many people who've come before us, arrows and wagon wheels, obsidian tools, buffalo. Look out at the meadow, you can almost see them, generations dissolved in the bluegrass and hay. I want to try and be terrific. Even for an hour."

I AM A POET, I AM A WOMAN

Life is by design.

Not everyone will play by the rules.

Just because someone is in your family doesn't mean they are nice, loving or kind.

Make sure you're comfortable with the end-result before you walk away.

I wish I could live this journey of

forever to share life with you.

SHEILA BRIDGES

"My definition of success has very little to do with other people's expectations."

I AM AN INTERIOR DESIGNER, I AM A WOMAN

ABIGAIL MARCELO

"Don't be afraid to be bold and be you!"

I AM AN INTERIOR DESIGNER, I AM A WOMAN

"We cling to our own point of view, as though everything depended on it. Yet our opinions have no permanence; like autumn and winter, they gradually pass away." - **Zhuangzi**

“Behold, my friends, the spring is come; the earth has gladly received the embraces of the sun, and we shall soon see the results of their love!” – **Sitting Bull**

"Live in the sunshine. Swim in the sea. Drink in the wild air." – **Ralph Waldo Emerson**

“My sorrow, when she’s here with me, thinks these dark days of autumn rain are beautiful as days can be; she loves the bare, the withered tree; she walks the sodden pasture lane.” - **Robert Frost**

"No other love in the world is like the love of a father has for his little girl."

ARTVOICES
BOOKS

Beyonce

Shakira

Salma Hayek

Viola Davis

Dr. Rebecca Crumpler

Constance Baker Motley

Carmen Ortiz

Sonya Sotomayor

Ketanji Brown Jackson

Angela Davis

Maria Elena Salinas

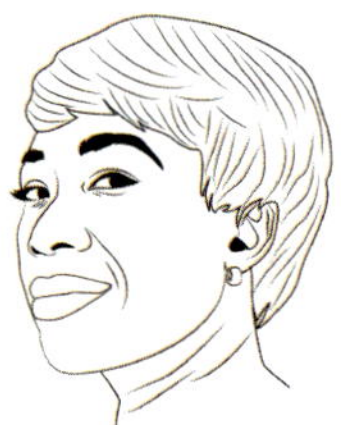

Joy Reid

Ann Lowe

Carolina Herrera

Ellen Ochoa

Katherine G Johnson

Sabrina Gonzalez Pasterski

Frida Escobedo

Norma Merrick Sklarek

Thelma Golden

Maria Teras Arnal

Mary Jackson

Bell Hooks

Gloria Anzaldua

Rita Pierson